T0267727

Cold Dogs

Cold Dogs

Zan de Parry

The Song Cave

The Song Cave
www.the-song-cave.com
Zan de Parry, 2024
Cover image: © Zan de Parry, 2024

Design and layout by Janet Evans-Scanlon

ISBN: 979-8-9878288-6-1
Library of Congress Cataloguing-in-Publication Data has been applied for.

FIRST PRINTING

Contents

For Chelsea

have you ever held a cat's jaw shut?
Brittle as ice.

—GEORGE STARBUCK

BANGING

I listen to my inner voice
It calls things by their inner names

Tridelt is short for delta delta delta
Triage is short for age age age
Chrysanthemum is christ unfolded

People, banging to history
People, blank as a trotter
People, linked at the waist
Children, play fair

THE SNAIL

I sat in the soft of your elbow
And baled your armpit hair
I sat in the soft of your knee
Drilled kisses under your foot
You didn't wipe my trail
It hardened, it wrinkled
You didn't crush me!
Though it felt grim under your foot

I dunk my dum dum
In tears, a snail infinitely small

PARSON'S NOSE

I'm doing healthy with
mommy and daddy.
There's tires all over the landscape here.
I ate a lot of red cereal and now
it's time for bed.
The look of attraction in a man's face
makes me sick.
That bone on the inside of your elbow
is called a parson's nose
and you have a big one.

WIPING

I take razor and gill my blue pearls
Hold your bone platter under my rounded arch
In only basketball the suits pick up the towels

Wiping means take a rag that has already been wiped with
The rag is yours, still damp from the last wipe
To wipe up whatever you do, good or bad

POEM OF LONGING

The dog sits
In his own autumn
Fills his nose
No stain
That old say-by:
I'll me too
On two off
In a row days
And kick high
The copper pot

ALUMINUM, TIN, NICKEL

I set a pick-stool, let it stand
Set upon it my tin hand
I let it clink, let it back
I let it clink again and crack
In the air the metal petals
Aluminum, tin, nickel

I set a pick-stool, let it stand
Set upon my tin hand
I let it clink, feel it sting
I let it clink again and ring

A box of things that say they're rubbers
A box of box that say it's knockers
In the air the metal petals
Aluminum, tin, nickel

NUCLEAR WAR

At the university there is a mysterious course
In which a black & white film begins with war
And ends with a dog biting a ball

A student says she's reminded
That the human body is mostly water

Another says she's reminded
Of the sermon Van Gogh wrote on a leaf

One of the class allies laughs
As though living a life subtracted from God

The teacher responds to the first
"In which heart sediment can be found"

The second
"Faith makes a man easy"

The third
"Well aren't you your own cup of twenty perspectives"

At the university there is a mysterious course
In which a black & white film begins with war
And ends with a dog biting a ball

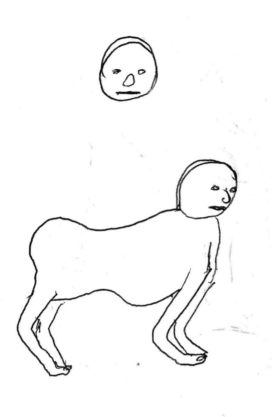

MY DOG

Plump
Long hair
Fangs
Short legs
Highway (former name)
Reversible
Erroneous
Insecure
Crying regularly
Me and my dog would eat grass together
Lie back and think
A bus could take us between towns
Through town
Even between states
And we go to sleep
Dream about tracks

AT SMOKER'S NECK

If my girl went
blind I would not
love her less.
Never say never
unless under duress.
Climb the spruce
& the smell of steppe.
Daddy king legs crawling
up her

bodenschatz
of brunette fleece

THE WHIMPER

If they ask me to eat this peacock
I will say eat, yes
And all the luck it was prepared with

WAS THAT A CARDINAL
OR HAVE I AN EYE CUNT

The milk, the eggs, the husks, the bones and the nuts
I eat the head, I eat the tail

I eat the heart, the lungs, the stomach, the intestines, the anus,
    the cloak,
the bladder, the prostate and the spleen

I'm eating the fur, eating the blood, eating the flesh, eating the fat,
eating the marrow, eating the bones, eating the shells,
eating the flesh of the eggs, eating the meat of the chicken,
eating the meat of the beef, eating the meat of the pork,
eating the meat of the fish, eating the meat of the crustaceans,
eating the marrow of the pulque, drinking the milk of the cow,
    of the pig

Drinking the milk of the child, drinking the milk of the bull,
    the milk of the sheep,
of the goat, drinking the milk of the chicken, drinking the milk
    of the pig,
drinking the milk of the turkey

I eat the tongue, the teeth, the nails, the skin, the skin of the paws,
    the claws,
the bones, the gallbladders, the bowels, the colon, the rectum,
    the pancreas,

the testicles, the ovaries, the testes, the scrotum, the anus,
the anus of the female, the anus of the male, the anus of all
the mammals,
the anus of everything, the anus, the anus

DID I EAT IT, ACTUALLY?

No, the thin wings of the soul remain paired
I am for the future
For the good and against all the bad
So, crossing into sight
A pre-teen ages in a turnaround
12. Years.
And asks me, looking at me
Ever heard of a workout?
Look, if sitting down is my mission
Why do I need to build a life around something else?

ALCOHOL

I never thought wine was alcohol
Because grapes come from the garden
A wasp in a petrol jar
An iguana
Jumping from a banana tree
Into a muddy creek

IF FEATHERS WERE CIGARETTES

This week I reunited with a friend
We ordered the same food
Bread with a simple sauce
She brought me metal pansies
She said there's a story in her family of a duck
Like all ducks this duck wore water
But didn't like the wetness
But burned her feathers
Rather than omitting the river
The conversation was difficult to hold
And somehow very expensive
I see myself as this duck I said

I THINK I WAS A SECRETARY

If there was a video I could pull from my memories
It would be a full winter day
If there was a hotline I could wire to my memories
The numbers would be anachronistic
The fire on Vinewood
Those white flies dying on our shoulders
I dreamt a wagon to be sold
A wagon
Or wood
Or something simply for fire
I logged the wagon and naturally moved on
I think I was a secretary

LORRAINE

I saw Lorraine on the TV show Sound Ring
She performed a song with words like
I want to touch the ocean
I want to touch the sand
What would happen if I got to the ocean
If I got in the water
I'm a reflective person who doesn't drive
I sing about the sun and moon to say
I know where the blood is spilled

DO NOT THINK THAT FIRE IS NOT
ABOUT YOU OR IT IS ALL FOR NOTHING

Fire applies to not only money and documents
But also wearable things
I stored one thing in two places and thankfully have something to wear
Even if money was at home
I would have pushed my gold so my photos wouldn't have disappeared
Now I understand hard-drives
Keeping bags is ridiculous
But in the morning bags were demanded
I don't appeal to those who round them up but no longer laugh
Be friends with neighbors and people in general!
Surround yourself with more than you are able to choose!
I want to bow to those who showed what it means to be human
Who talked over the fire that silently looked to kill us
Who left, came back in a midnight pale with NOs for answers
Who offered life
Whose milky lives we flooded with ashy sacks

OCTAVIAN

I sit flat and sit languidly
watching spiders dip their human grub
in the crystal calm next to me
dual consumers photographing guineas
beyond the biting markers on the dangers of applause
and sprigged amongst this deepest green,
wild African rose, white Bulgarian hopiate:
one standout tent swallow.
If I say that I couldn't sing
And if I sang . . .
If I say that I couldn't bring
And if I brang . . .
If I say that I couldn't swim
And if I swame . . .
forgetting about living, forgetting about living,
and those other wonderful thoughts
that drift through my head?
This morning, at three, Octavian, an acquaintance,
called to say that he loved me.

CAMPER'S SOCK

Patience with a stronger body
Come out, don't be shy
Hiding in the cranberries
Lacking crankshaft armor
If I love you, you love me
A truth too heavy
To be hung in a camper's sock

CRUEL EXTENSIONS

I enter the shop of an absent grocer to steal
The door behind me closes and secures
I try to break the door with a rack
I break the window onto my face
The owner catches me in my climb
And pulls me down to kick me in the head
I'm no prisoner to walking
I walked into the cage of walking willingly
I've touched every ad, become brilliantly traceable
Ate food wrapped in bright words as if the food itself could speak
Yesterday I got shot with footprints in my face
The king pulled me down
And kicked me in the head with power
At first I was upset
Because it seemed to reflect the essence
Of what keeps happening
But I don't want to write like that
I want to live a long, good, hard, young life

THE FARMER

A hell of a hell
It's hard to fight fucked up
Well, let's get strong and pull the belts down
Mentally I'm from the north
My hands hang with pounds of jewelry
Here are the photos, some stuck together
Because in my youth it was hot
I've already said it once
That when I'm in the bath I think of a six foot nail
Just about to go in
So today I've got to say it twice
It's time to say it three times
Oh, there goes my life

HAY

For Bradley

Just today
Walking out of hay
I came here to do hay
Bag some corn
I noticed that the wild
Malva was admiring
A forgotten blooming
Overgrown and unfulfilled
Mercilessly unloved
At the gas station crossing
The dawn threshold
Beyond the green chickens
There are still lonely fields
Painfully maintained

BARN DOOR

You can buy pants with pockets
On the pants. I use these for trips
To pocket-sized places, like my historic homeland
I've long realized that keeping my phone in my pocket
Is cost-effective, like living in a barn
Crack open your phone and see
Two people wearing glasses having sex

I can't wait to take you home and rob you
Break your chaste and taste it with masa
To get a piece of your galore
Show up out of the woods at like 1000 AM
Cook you a boiling plate within seven minutes
Add 25 dollars to a new savings account
Until I can afford you an old, beautiful bridge

EVAN & EVE

When the great ocean stood
Her water fell off
And made the ocean

When the ocean stood
Her water fell off
And made the great lake

When the great lake stood
Her water fell off
And made the lake

In middle-night
In glass brassier
My reflection
In the creek

STEALING & SWEARING

All problems are hunger
Stealing is the anthem of hunger
Don't starve your hunger
Ribs are the rims of coins
Don't share with children
Defy instinctive continuation of kind
Dear my shortest words
You probably got pleasure from insulting people
Forging rifle permits
Running through the market on cattle
I replace "fuck" with "Kubota Station"
"O fuck" with "I was at Kubota Station"

LUMBO

My father, a hard worker
Pushed us into every direction of town
He's still there, which I find intrepidly slow
I, however, am taking my time
Patient to the annual faricy
Being Known Might Be Greatest Possible Achievement

A very-haired thus well-shadowed man
My father painted America's modern landscape
And only in a day, enchanted by the speaking-nature of Americans
How they act when they enact
The brazen, the lazy, the freaks of consciousness

Tell me, vacant creatures
What it is to be ill-feeling
To be naked and puny
How it is to be hyper-grand-feeling
Over something undeveloped

AMERICAN SUICIDE

I like the light smell of deer
The sounds of singing
I don't like crowds or clusters

My favorite place on the bus
The middle door, ear
To the bus middle door glass

Flaggers, before raising it
Hold it and blow it
Armstrong blew his to the moon

TRAIN TO UZHGOROD

The men are shit!
The women foaming fish!
The children, mendicants
The coldness of the mountains
Enters the sunlight of the East
And the Russian King eats off his daisy
But Uzhgorod is beautiful
The fields, the river, the carnival in the woods
The smart scout and his huge head
Tender salo
O saint, o saint one can never expect!
Your composer lights my rotting fuse!
Children drink with me under a bridge!
America phones-in number-questions
Hnhh!
Shape your cottageless organ America
I'll be in Uzhgorod

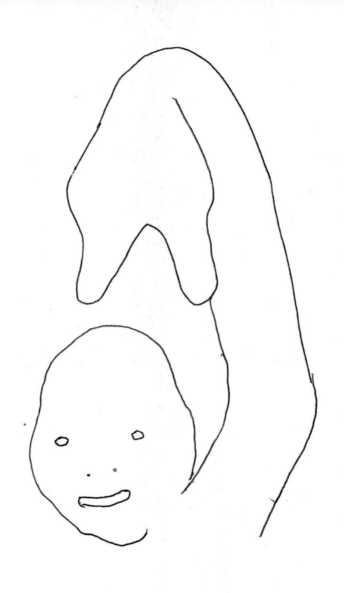

THE DEPUTY

A neighbor boy to whom the man was confidante
Spoke on a nuance to his washing
I suds what I sees, when I shower I suds nothing
And when I bath I suds the front half
Beleaguered by this approach
The man demanded the boy's mother aware
He didn't hold the boy's hand any different
They didn't walk any different
And with the same plan as yesterday
Sit in the yard and ask what that looks like
What does that look like, and what's that?
The mother, a deputy, arrived in a brown, high car
With a green star on the door
The man asked the boy to hold tight
Keep asking questions I need to speak with your mother
And so it became over two warm mugs
Have you heard anything on your son's washing?
My son's washing? Why would I've heard anything on that?
The man asked the mother if one day the boy appeared cleaner
    than another
But by the willowing of her eyes was told she was not this sort
    of deputy

DEAR MR. d

Dear Mr d.
Please respond.
I want to send you an envelope
with a prayer and a kilo of love
for saving from tears
one beautiful boy.
You picked the love
out of my chest
and it grew into a
common experience.
Over my lifetime
the clown has grown new fingers
and a pair of tendrils
yet nothing yet is known
about the face.
Dear Mr d.
Please respond.
I want to send you an envelope
with a prayer and a kilo of love
for saving from tears
one beautiful boy.
You picked the love
out of my chest
and it grew into a common experience.
Over my lifetime
the clown has grown new fingers

and a pair of tendrils
yet nothing yet is known
about the face.
A gylant siren
with sfire for eyes.

JOHN THE CONQUEROR

At four and a half I got a new baby
A little brother
And if I did something bad
He'd see my mother beat me with her hissing strap
Strap-prints remained for a week
First red, then blue, then purple
But I was a healthy mare
"Gotta watch the little one"
If he did anything bad like me
I was afraid to even imagine the consequences
But I became uninterested in that
And started to read
But brother . . . brother was an active child
Yes. He was

PETER

I approach a seller
The man seems a Peter
He is selling colored shovels, wine, slippers shaped like sheep
Despite the suspicious clouds he appears sun-drunk
I notice a baby between his feet
I pick up the baby in horror from Peter
Where is his doctor? His mother? What are his needs?
Perhaps there are photos tucked with him?
He has wasted himself
His legs begin to thicken
He continues to thicken all over, gaining in smell
I begin to be carried
I begin to be chased
I'm chased by the baby with an axe and fuel
He's scary as shit, unpredictable
When I pull out my cross he kind of stops
I didn't think it would work but it kind of does
I walk to the church to tell the bishop
He runs to archives to tell the books

PROSTATE CANCER

My friend's father told me once ago
He worked at some plant on some farm land
The plant was engaged in the production of plastic products
And it was a great surprise for me to learn
That the plant was quite healing, loved its employees
At the plant there was an amazing dining room
Whose chef once decided that the remaining food waste
Would be good to feed to something else
For example, chickens
SO HE BUILT A COOP
And the eggs were fresh
Then the 90s came
The dining room ceased to be so gorgeous
That chef retired
Nothing to feed the chickens, decided to get rid of them
And, as the storyteller swore
As everyone watched that old coop get razed
Something even strong plant men could not endure
Bald, skinny, eyeballlless, beakless appearances of hell, but shorter
And one acrid freak of a cock

I LET THE TERRORIST TOUCH MY HEAD

He had drawn an old woman with a crutch
It was like a page from a fairytale
He was smiling at me
I know you from somewhere, he said
I looked at him, wondering where he was from
I looked at the drawing again
A depiction of an old woman with a crutch
Where do you live? I asked
The library, he said
The spies were still following him
The library, I said. Where is the library?
I looked at the drawing again
I recognized it from the cover of a magazine
on the shower chair in the bathroom
Right here, he said
He gently folded my head into my chest
And my face into my groin
Friend, let me show you an informal way
to achieve dreams

THE ORANGE CAT

In the fairy tale The Orange Cat
We raise Jesus to what suffices
We make Jesus IDs, cars, phones
A home the size of the United Nations
And we warm him with beautiful song

We tattoo to his breasts, do not eat your neighbors
To save yourselves, and in his name
Construct an equal-opportunity bunkhouse
Filled with warm hay and fox down
A quarter-home out back
For the didacts to smoke frankincense

Jesus is not our king
An unseen king is an unfit king
Though as we make construction of divination
An orange cat always seems to pass
A cat whose paws we nail to spare timber
So that an image of a king might pool under it

THE SALESMAN

I'm not sure where this myth of snake oil
Being unhealthy came from
I have seen people make snake oil by hand
With the snake fruit from the snake tree
One pack of stamps with initials made
In hand-embossing technique
Italian leather, vegetable braid
2.5mm thickness
The case painted in red and maroon waves
Covered in naturally-tight waxes
Edged in Spanish gray soap
A bunch of dead ends that can't be circumvented
Shifting lines with infinity to infinity tied in a bow

INFINITE TAPS

You have a desire to achieve something—you go to study
Study well—you have a job
Dream of becoming even better—study further
You learn well—you have a very good job
You have a job and a head on your shoulders—you go to different
    measures
You go to the event—you meet people who distribute survey ads
    under the ploys
You don't listen to your friend who tells you not to drag it all home
You drag it all home
When you drag everything home—do not open the door
Some of you are proud—and that shakes me

TOTAL LOSS & DISORDER

Do you remember when I found that fleece pantalone?
Real ones, like grandmother's?
Well, it deceived me
I had to feel it, turn it inside out, and I, as I saw
Saw that the pantalone was synthetic
After washing first thing it electrocuted me
Secondly, it is not a pantalone at all, but shorts
Even half of the carriage does not close
Stretched broad but nipped in length
Thirdly, it has a very strange carriage
Even here it is awkward to say
That it doesn't look like a carriage at all
Like on a normal underwear
It's not otherwise to think us men have neglected forms
But at the cunt should be a welded iron?

COPPER ANNIVERSARY

You woke today with a joyful exclamation
I have grown another wisdom tooth!
Soon again screams from the kitchen
Our milk is gone bad! No, our porridge is spoiled!
I'm sippin' I'm sippin' and she's not thick at all!
I wish my legs were long like yours
So that when we ride the carousel
I could drag them through the bushes

I'm often talked to by strangers on the street
Today's case is the best so far
By the playground, a voice from behind
Woman! A woman! Way to go!
I looked around just in case there's a friend
Yes, yes, I'm talking to you!
Tell me, how many children have walked on that playground?

I read that this year's our copper anniversary
I will ask for a copper penis as a gift, to stir jam
Maybe next year a lot of fruit will grow at the cottage?

YOU

You grew through the awl hole
of the virginal garment
and in a wave of unbounded relief
thank the ruling counsel
and laugh with the upper world
I come home prayed
Yet to start a great fast
Fingers slotting through my skin wounds
Announcement of wonder (faith)
I don't want anything anymore
Only you
(Drops faith)
God is sweet, but you are a loon's eye,
blythe and ignored, blocking the face
of that old, framed mank
You, who were born in 1966
The main thing in a most beautiful opera
The only one with all three simulacra
sowed into your mandolin
as some kind of reliquary . . .

HONEY GUMBALLS

I wake in the evening, realize that I am dead
Lie around like a grain drill, greedily drink water to orgasm
I move slow and calculated as if yesterday I slapped my neighbor
Or smoked-up mama's wooden house, no less
Fighting for life, moaning, He's a hero, He's a warrior
He put His hand on boob and fell asleep?
And if, God forbid, my night-way
From the back door to the
Bed doesn't go through
Will you look at me
In the eyes and say, dictating:
Lo, I rock for you
My long island dove.
I twist for you

VERTIGO

Your thighs
From the bowling biltong
Walking
In the shudder
Of a blue drape
In a sensible world
Vertigo
Is a plant
Your brain is sweets
And I want to make smarts to it

VIBRAPHONE

Your cubbage
Has me quandariless
Inside them jeans
I find what you walk with to me
A bount
Unquestionably bouffant
That level, par précis
After sex over
You I pray
Trapezoidally

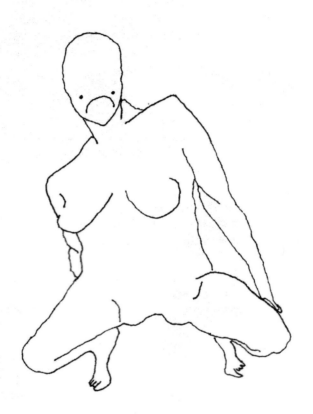

RESUSCATIVE

In that shit-dark hamlet
She picked me up by my backstory
And got into it, arms malfigured by angle
Black lines of squirted rubber on the wall
Hit by the flash
That was her invective against my wont
She won
Voice pregnant as anything with an uglier version of itself
It passed, noncompetitively
As so this contest in personal loss

THIS IS INCREDIBLE

In the pass they met
She in black beret with pigeon strips
A four-gown visual weight
He a white sleeve floating over a blow
Sort of heater
Impressing eventual travel
Are you warming?
Warm's hard for such a thin thing
She flapped up a layer, tell me minister
Why float all night in this covered pass
Then rattle off at the moon
The tune

VERONICO

When I return home from a nightly walk
And greet his breast with my hand at his house
I don't notice the car rolling by
Dear, why are you touching the monument?
Glory, I tell them
Glory, from the Toyota
Holding his black grape bouquet
For the carpenters
For the fragrant red flowers
Of my bucegarine
Nearby, you say
At the shooting range
There is a well?
The river has dried up
And
In this time of no water
I ask for your tears, Veronico

THING YOU DO

One of the girls in the band
And this is a younger group
Plays a huge synth
And so inspired and emotional
Though mostly just presses that demo tune button
But supposedly can play the keys
With the expression of a world class pianist
And the band is led by a 72-year-old nurse
Doing her exercises
Who squats, waves her hands
And yells for you to bring her a towel
But for it to be small
And to have the hook loop sewn
Not somewhere
But in the middle of the long side
And you sit and suffer from where to get it
Then sew it
And you climb into the closet with all of the junk
Where there's a small towel
With a loop
Not nowhere
But right in the middle of the long side

PATHETICUS

for poachers

PATHETICUS, let's calm down a little bit, stop the game.
I'll get you the chaplain, she'll bring you some cognac...
What? Why would I...
I'll give you her number.
What! Why would you . . .
PATHETICUS . . .
Think about the kid's dinky one-watt light bulb.
The only reason the light is on is because we keep pressing the button.
Where does the light go?
Into the kid's heart, into a mass of parasympathetic fibres.
That's the source of the light. That's the computer.
Nothing inside the bulb. Nothing under it.
When you step onto the concrete platform
squeeze-in tight between the cables
and breathe into the mask. Your mother will pull the lever,
and the platform will slowly drop into the hole.
Not really. I'm a servant at the palace. For the King!
PATHETICUS . . .
Your first words came out the moment you were born.
You said, "my life is in your hands."

IF IT'S IN THE HEAD IT FITS

The author of Wicca. Born in London.
Spent his childhood and adolescence in the United States
where he had to deal with McCarthy
who was from the late 18th century and born to a farmer called "Rutt"
At the gate to his barn a statue of a young woman
donated by the pupils of the Royal School 4 Drama and Drama
accompanied by a stone tablet which displays the name "Duke"
On a white wicker chair
fishes alone
Jamey "The Rest of the Story" Harris

SOMETIMES YOU MUST PUT A PERSON
INTO THE ABSENCE OF A FRAME

She was a beautifully old lady
Yellow gloves, umbrella, a veil
She laughed in an accent
But when I touched her hand it must have broken her
She started to joke poisonously and laugh at herself

He was an uncle
Asked a question
Answered himself
Offended himself
Called himself "hazel grouse"

She was a young woman crying with happiness
I'm not lying
She said she was happy!
Good thing I finished early
I can remove the deer from the garden
And go home in sin!

It was close to morning
The hypers were asleep
The room felt large
She asked with understanding
Aren't you tired? This one who's stood all night?

THE RESTAURANT

I walk into the light of an empty restaurant
I like its stupid look
I walk by a table near the bar
I circle the table
A chef drums his fingers on a menu
Hello, this is a restaurant, right?
Three children join me
Three more menus
Forks, knives, spoons, more napkins?
Ye, we're not in a hurry
We do everything slow
Easing the moment into its fittings

This is not steak
As steak is bigger, thicker
And is not made of pork
It's not a cutlet
Because it hasn't been beaten
It's not steak because "steak" is beef
This is not escalope, as escalope
Is prepared from the pup's blade
This is not a pork locket
As it is a medallion itself

I don't know what they did to the chicken
But it was pale and slick

The sheep seemed ok
I didn't do the pork
The pita I liked
Mostly because it was covered in a "haze sauce"
The homemade white wine was good
The check above average
Two snacks, one main dish
Two wines and a tea in a can
The slick chicken in my stomach
And the waiter's running, laughing

We went to eat at a restaurant
And were a bit shocked by the quality
For example, the prawn cocktail
Was not cooked at all
There was the hummus
Rather like tomato soup
Served with arroz con culo
And an appetizer of ikiri-zushi, a fillet
With an ice cream top
A few glasses of red wine did not
Quiet the rumors
And on the gravel, in the lot
Children were setting fire
To a box of live crabs

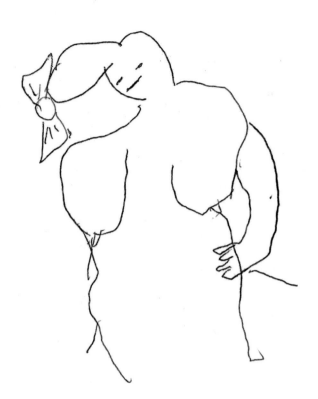

ANGELS

Angels can burn off their wings
Lose their championships of life
Leave the divine house
Smoke cigarettes
Start over
Should they so desire
A café filled with words like
Tranquility
Northern Lights
Pizza
Hot Café
Coffee-that

.

MORGAN

You look like a morgan
Excuse me I says
And looks out the window
For morgans

You look like a marble
Excuse me I says
And pulls out my marble
My cat's eye

RESEMBLE THE TITANS

"Where did you come from my love?"
And the mop of her hair goes all the way down
Even Knievel's
Time, that old bum
Middle name was "Peace"
I'm drinking brother I'll tell you like a madman
There's nothing substandard about being unrealistic for a long time
I wanted to get something unique for my girlfriend's birthday
So I got her a drugged-out hug
1. She loved it
2. She loved that I got a deal on it

DEAR BUDDIES ROLLING OUT:

even when May didn't flirt
or Laura aka Ross didn't sing
Disordered eating.
I say good –
She yells start.
The single pale in which Peer Pan sailed his world
eggs
by gunshot the man commat suicide;
he is abruptly clueless:
Today, missed 2 really romantic thunderstorms
across America.

COMMON ENEMY

Corporations are attempts by legal persons to redo human traits
I turn to leaders who have been developing these traits
I am on the crest of their wave
I monitor their trends
I am responsible
I will not lag
I am used to being a leader
Sleeping in parks and landfills
Changing in transit-hut windows
Tapping our common enemy on the shoulder

CRAB THEORY

There is a very interesting thing called crab theory
Theory of buckets of crabs

Crabs are selfish shells who together
Can leave a bucket, though try alone, cooking

As a boy leaving drugs:
Friends say it won't work, stretching the drugs—crab bucket

As a high school girl
Colleagues loudly wonder: why do you need it?
All the work—crab

When strangers call you their desired words it is the same
Curve of the bucket

We can suppose
This is human nature
And it does not help

COLD DOGS

I thought nothing
Could anything the shit out of anything else

But here
Cold dogs stacking up in the yard

Bare, mother
Arch within arch you bleed between them

LEASH OF JOY

I'm stressful today

Tripped over an erect mop
Cut my hand very bad
Literally shifted the whole meat

Ran around the kitchen
Pouring very precious blood
Stood at a threshold and

Ma, am I okay?

I'd come out to a sky
In a fur coat
Broken-in by a thin soul

Can you imagine?

LIKO & FUN

Yesterday I saw Liko & Fun walking on the bridge
Their comments aren't interesting at all
They're funny, not smart, precisely why they bully
There's no rule when crossing a bridge
To just pass without shooting somebody down

I could see the raise of dividing rings in his all-proof gloves

He made a seven with his hands
Pointed at himself, a three with a hand
Pointed at me

What's wrong kid, no self-respecto?

THE DOG

The dog is in the fortress living on Earth
Doesn't need spas or sails
Here he's washed with p-water
Slept, put on a couple cubes of firewood
The internet is shitty
Less amenities than a house
Tell me, dog
How much money do you need for happiness?
For full happiness?
Six thousand four hundred!?
So tormented by this question . . .
Is this what you need for complete happiness? To leave the fortress?
Delouse your gray braids and collect berries?
Thick eyebrows with elegant eye bags
White pants from Brazil
You want to rob royal ships and swim with the bartenders?
Eat nothing for a very long time and then . . .
And then?
Is heaven fair?
Do wolves share leashes?
You won't get your neptune
Eating the cherry out of a sailor's belly button!

THE MISSIONARY

Flies draw hexagons around my neck
Butterflies dust flowers to get lost
I don't want to die fighting the cross
My poor clothes drinking my blood
Drinking American milk is to hire the archer
To bring shortening blades at our future
Never date the doctor who makes medicine jokes

It is 2020 and I am Catholic
I pick my dog up like a man when the hawks fly over
A parrot named Blue cracks a dark nut on a wet jungle stone
I wake to flush my luminal sac
Drink too much or underline too much in The Watchtower
I did a lot of whips from the checks
I made a chair for the cheeks
What's a couple sunny shoulders?

The hole I puts my head in
The hole my head comes out of
I wish I still lived in the can times
I can do this, I put my money into a can
A mountain chalet on a nape of the world
Old oak furniture, animal skins
Acolytes at the fireplace
Luca, playing *Parade Personelle,* naked

I can't wait to die so you and I can go haunting
Every time I go hunting I go missing
Life is easy, and other shepherd's lies
Jupiter is just balled-up pants in the astronomer's eye
A coat with a kimono in it
A coma with candles on the arms
Strike the match with extra stuff at the end
A dream is a dream until you see it

THE PENETRALIUM

In the center of the sanctum is a penetralium of the darkness below
Noy, man, I could look to the gear to the penetralium if you would just
    speak the word
So into the penetralium they toppled me, clapping down the shutter
    and its latch above
"The penetralium," Cooder shuddered, and a color rose up from his
    face
The garden contained a penetralium, into which the missus, while
    walking, fell
The games went on, still nothing would please some of the young ones
But we should see the penetralium

YOU EVER WONDER
HOW SHELLSHOCK WORKS?

You are fresh as a bird
Fresh from the egg
With the shell-top still
On your head

When somebody yells
What's happening, what's happening
And we all start happening
Together

ACHIEVEMENTS OF THE UNLOCKED

Ambivalence hands ambivalence to ambivalence
Making an ambivalent chain
While I stand waist deep
In the substructure
There's a little thing inside you
That looks like you
When you tell betraying stories

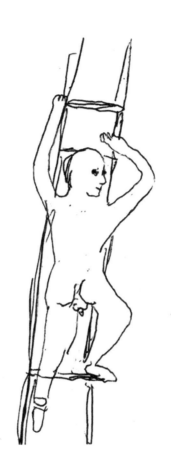

THE SERMON

Life, as I've known it
Is a creature tended to halt
Belief in its own stigma that
Increasing life increases life
Increases money, increases passionately
Your love for anything else

To be born is to take time
To pair with another
Break then remember
Every day is a new day
For sticking to guns
And showing up

If you live long enough
And pay close enough attention
You will see that your energy
Your truest human resource
Finds all motivation
Sexually attractive

CAVE SWIFTLET

You call me by phone
You saw me on rat hay cam
Jumping, landing on coiled copper
Bringing something to someone
Like a criminal in a private territory
I address you in three languages
My grandfather's pearls
A couchette wagon
Our life of thirty equal years
A woman in a field of sunflowers
A brunette with these flowers
Here, flower-loving girl

WITHIN THE GENERAL PUBLIC
IS A PSEUDO PUBLIC

I don't want to read the news anymore
I don't want to read about kids, drunken incidents
Body parts
I don't want to think about the body
Like I think about the parts
Perhaps religion has lied about angels
I inspect them
Anyways
I've lost you to where you can't be found

MOVIE THE SIZE OF A DECK OF CARDS

Perfect weather in sleeves rolled up
Sort of from doing something earlier
If the trees looked at men
The way men look at women
We'd never get out of these woods
Midwestern men are gross, they say
Men are bad, they say
Ever get in a fight with one?
The responsibility for your own life
Floats just outside the body
You simply need to sign it home

MOVIE THE SIZE OF A DECK OF CARDS

The veins of my chest turned up
As a blue spectacle of hands covering each other
Soap was yellow still on you
Grown-up date flavor
The night kept saying a glowing us, shall we say
Us! can you hear it?
The babe singing mama
In his papa's arms?
The beat
Of his little detail???

COLLECTING STONES

I pick up a stone and take it to my face.
I hold it with my mouth and out for the cat to lick, and the cat licks it.
She looks at me in a confused way and scratches me.
I look at her in a confused way and she scratches me again.
I put my head on her chest and sigh, kiss her on the cheek
and she blushes, and I make her laugh.
I pick my nose and stretch it out with my teeth.
Sometimes, in bed, I will kiss my brother on the lips.
Sometimes I kiss my sisters on the lips.
My legs look too long to run but I will run them in the dark.
I will work in a factory, yes, yes.
I will finish university, yes, yes.
I will have a family, yes, yes.
I will fall in love with somebody else, yes, yes.
I will stand for the national anthem, yes, yes.
I will blow a kiss to the flag, yes, yes.
I will sway with you and the baby, yes, yes.
I will leave, yes.
I will live to be an old man, yes, yes, yes, yes.
I will be accepted as a woman, yes, yes.
I will look into the face of a woman, yes.
I will look into the face of another woman, yes.
I have picked the lock without breaking a sweat.
I walk to the river to wash. I bring a chair and a water pot.
There are a thousand tarantella.
I let them climb the chair to the pot and jump to my shoulders.

I let them dry themselves with my hair.
A beautiful girl comes to the chair.
She came from the song, "I Love You, My Love."
She opens her mouth, the tea in it is my mother's.
She cries, *So many tarantella!*
She sings:
O Zanny boy
My Swedish fish
My little girl
Your darling ways
I see your face
O Zanny boy
O Zanny boy
Please watch your ways
I see your life
I see so fake
I like your eyes
Sweet Zanny boy
Sweet Zanny boy

Acknowledgments

To the fast fat kids, deserters, arable land, competition, mink, ecoterrorists, telehandlers, people with my current phone number, spinster mechanics curled up on the cold slab, event rental business, lake tides, collective eye of heaven. To The Song Cave and whoever led us here. Thank you.

OTHER TITLES FROM THE SONG CAVE: